THE
GRAVEDIGGER

A FRANKENSTEIN STORY

This is a work of fiction. All of the characters, events, and organizations portrayed in this work are either products of the authors' imagination or used fictitiously.

The Gravedigger - A Frankenstein Story

ISBN-13: 978-0692347980
ISBN-10: 0692347984

For information about production rights, visit:
www.jzettelmaier.com

Published by Sordelet Ink

THE GRAVEDIGGER
A FRANKENSTEIN STORY

A PLAY BY

JOSEPH ZETTELMAIER

INSPIRED BY THE NOVEL BY

MARY SHELLY

Published by
Sordelet Ink

The Gravedigger: A Frankenstein Story was originally produced as a joint premiere between First Folio Theatre (Oak Brook, IL) and Williamston Theatre (Williamston, MI) in October of 2014.

First Folio Theatre's production was directed by Alison C. Vesely. Stage Managed by Sara Gammage. Sound Composed and Designed by Christopher Kriz. Costume Design by Rachel Lambert. Lighting Design by Michael McNamara. Scenic Design by Angela Weber Miller. Prop Design by Cassy Shillo. Fight Choreography by Joe Foust. Melanie Keller was the Assistant Director. The cast was as follows:

KURT: Craig Spidle
VICTOR: Doug MacKechnie
ANTON: Joshua Carroll
NADYA: Simina Contras

The understudies were David Rice (KURT), T. Isaac Sherman (VICTOR), Ben Muller (ANTON) and Yesmeen Mikhail (NADYA).

Williamston Theatre's production was directed by John Lepard. Stage Managed by Stefanie Din. Scenic Design by Kirk A. Domer. Lighting Design by Daniel C. Walker. Costume Design by Karen Kangas-Preston. Prop Design by Bruce Bennett. Sound Design by Michelle Raymond. Fight Choreography by Zev Steinberg. The cast was as follows:

KURT: Mark Colson
VICTOR: Joe Seibert
ANTON: Alex Leydenfrost
NADYA: Alysia Kolascz

Cast of Characters

VICTOR ~ the Doctor
KURT~ the Gravedigger
ANTON ~ the Monster
NADYA ~ a gypsy

Time

The Late 1700s

Place

A cemetery outside of Ingolstadt, Bavaria

ACT I

Scene One

(Lights up. KURT's small shack. VICTOR sits at the table, waiting for KURT to return. Thunder is heard peeling in the distance. The door flies open. KURT enters. He is a large, strong man in his late 40s. He walks with a pronounced limp, leaning on his cane. He has a burlap sack slung over his shoulder. KURT starts at the sight of VICTOR)

KURT
Dammit all to hell! What are you doing here?

VICTOR
It's raining.

KURT
Of course it's raining! Been raining every day for a week.

VICTOR
You have them then?

KURT
I do.

VICTOR
Good.

(KURT drops the sack onto the table. It is large, and whatever's inside is heavy)

KURT
Pay me.

VICTOR
In good time.

KURT
Not "in good time." Now!

(KURT advances on VICTOR. VICTOR produces a knife. KURT stops)

KURT
So that's how it is, then? I dirty my hands for you, and you cut my throat?

(VICTOR stares at him, then cuts the tie-string on the sack. He looks inside)

KURT
Don't open it here. The stink...

VICTOR
...is something men like you and I should be used to.

(VICTOR looks inside, examining his merchandise. KURT mutters to himself)

KURT
Christ help me.

(VICTOR examines the merchandise, then ties the bag back up)

VICTOR
Well done.

KURT
Hmmm.

(VICTOR speaks as he examines)

VICTOR
What happened to your leg?

KURT
God.

VICTOR
What?

KURT
God happened.

VICTOR
Indeed?

KURT
Sometimes, we pay for our sins even before we die. You might want to think on that.

VICTOR
I might. But I don't.

(VICTOR takes out a sack of coins, & sets them on KURT's table)

KURT
I'm done.

VICTOR
Yes?

KURT
Yes. Find what you need from some other poor bastard. I can't do this anymore.

VICTOR
A little late for a weak stomach, don't you think?

KURT
This job's all I have. I can't risk it, no matter how much you pay me.

VICTOR
So that's it? A fear of unemployment? I'd thought it might be something more...substantial.

(KURT hobbles to the door, opening it)

KURT
Get out.

VICTOR
(Pointing to KURT's leg) I could have a look at that sometime. If you'd like.

KURT
No, I wouldn't like. Get out.

VICTOR
I am a doctor, whatever else you might think of me.

KURT
I'd rather not think of you at all.

VICTOR
You may be causing undue stress on your good leg, trying to overcompensate for your limp. If the brace isn't properly aligned...

KURT
I don't want your help.

VICTOR
Please. I don't like to see a man suffer.

(KURT can tell he genuinely means it. He softens his attitude & takes an old rosary from his pocket. He absently holds it as he speaks)

KURT
The damage is already done.

VICTOR
I'm sorry.

(KURT shrugs)

VICTOR
If it's any solace, the work I'm doing may one day make you whole again.

KURT
I'll pray for the day, sir, but not expect it.

VICTOR
Just know that...the work you've done for me... great good shall come of it.

(Beat)

KURT
You know what they call men like me? Resurrection men. Families come into a graveyard, see the dug-up plots...like their loved one's been resurrected. Except that's not it, is it? They've just been defiled. By men like me.

VICTOR
I won't bother you again. You have my word.

KURT
Thank you.

VICTOR
Well, then...

(VICTOR offers his hand to KURT. After a moment, KURT shakes it. VICTOR starts to leave)

KURT
God watch over you, Doctor.

VICTOR
Hmm. What an archaic notion.

(VICTOR exits. KURT takes out a flask and takes a long drink. Lights change)

Scene Two

(A year later. Lights up. The graveyard. A pile of dirt lies outside. KURT enters, limping worse. He's a bit drunk, and singing **Gaudeamus Igitur***)*

KURT
Gaudeamus igitur
Juvenes dum sumus.
Post iucundam iuventutem
Post molestam senectutem
Nos habebit humus.

(He stops at the dirt pile, preparing to urinate into the grave. He looks down)

KURT
Hey! What's this then?

(He sees a man lying in the open grave)

KURT
You! Get out of there.

(No response)

KURT
I know you can hear me! I said out!

(No response)

KURT
You asleep? Huh?!

(KURT pours his flask in the hole. ANTON speaks from within the hole)

KURT
Rise and shine, little dumpling.

ANTON
Leave me alone.

KURT
Ah! There! Now get out.

ANTON
No.

KURT
This hole's got a coffin going in it tomorrow. Sleep it off somewhere else.

ANTON
I'm not drunk.

KURT
More's the pity.

(KURT circles the hole, trying to figure out how to get down inside it)

ANTON
What are you doing?

KURT
I can't get down there on my own. So do an old sot a favor and...

ANTON
LEAVE ME BE!!!

KURT
Don't you shout at me! This is my damned bone-yard!

ANTON
Let me die in peace!

KURT
Oh no. No, no, no.

ANTON
Please!

KURT
This place isn't for the dying; it's for the dead.

ANTON
I'm begging you.

KURT
I'm sorry, but...

(ANTON begins to cry)

KURT
Oh. Oh. None of that.

(ANTON lets out a roar of anguish and rage. KURT staggers back. As ANTON rants, he crawls out of the hole)

ANTON
All I want is to die! My whole wretched life, it is the only thing anyone wished on me! And now. NOW...I am stopped!?

(ANTON is fully out of the hole. He is a large man, his face mostly wrapped in bandages. Only his

mouth and eyes are fully visible)

KURT
Oh my God...

ANTON
Why?! Why can't you just leave me be, and let me die?!

(KURT has fallen to his knees)

KURT
Please...please no...

ANTON
What are you...?

KURT
I'll go. I swear. Just don't hurt me. I'm begging you.

(ANTON's rage diminishes)

ANTON
I won't hurt you.

KURT
I'm sorry I shouted at you. I...

ANTON
Listen to me. I said I won't hurt you.

(He walks towards KURT. KURT tries to back away. ANTON reaches down and helps KURT stand)

KURT
What...?

(ANTON starts to leave. For reasons even he's unsure of, KURT speaks)

KURT
What happened to you?

(ANTON stops)

ANTON
I am...damaged.

KURT
Do you need help?

ANTON
No one can help me.

KURT
That's why you want to die.

(ANTON says nothing)

KURT
Perhaps I can help you.

ANTON
Why?

KURT
Because...I used to help people.

ANTON
Why?

KURT
It's what people do.

ANTON
No. It isn't.

KURT
Well...it's what we're supposed to do.

(They stare at each other for a bit)

KURT
Come with me.

ANTON
Where?

KURT
I have a shack, just past that mausoleum.

(ANTON doesn't move)

KURT
Come on. It's going to rain.

ANTON
Rain doesn't bother me.

KURT
Well, it bothers me. And I don't intend to leave you out here.

(Beat)

ANTON
You...don't want to leave me?

KURT
No. I suppose not.

(ANTON is silent for a while, taking that in)

ANTON
I'll go with you.

KURT
All right then.

(KURT leads the two of them off. Lights change)

Scene Three

(KURT's shack. KURT enters, followed by ANTON)

KURT
And...here we are.

(ANTON looks around)

ANTON
It is small.

KURT
Well, I was going to take you to my mansion, but I prefer my dingy shack ans its rustic charm. *(Beat)* That was a joke.

ANTON
I...I don't understand jokes.

KURT
I see.

(KURT hobbles to his chair and sits. He pulls out his flask, and offers it to ANTON)

ANTON
No.

(KURT drinks)

KURT
You don't have to just stand there.

(ANTON sits. He stares at a painting on the wall)

ANTON
Who is that? Your father?

KURT
Father of all of us, I guess. Saint Anthony.

ANTON
Your father was a saint?

KURT
No, but...old Anthony up there. He's the Patron
Saint of many things. Including gravediggers.

*(ANTON says nothing, continuing to stare at the
painting)*

KURT
Not one for conversation, are you?

ANTON
No.

(They sit in silence for a bit)

KURT
So what's your name?

ANTON
I have none.

KURT
You don't remember your name?

ANTON
I was never given one to remember.

KURT
You're putting me on.

ANTON
No.

KURT
Well, what do people call you?

(ANTON shrugs. KURT rubs his eyes in frustration)

KURT
What the hell am I supposed to call you then?
Hmm!?

(Again, ANTON shrugs)

KURT
Just pick something, will you? A name you like.
Anything.

ANTON
I don't know many names. And the ones I know,
I do not want.

KURT
All right then...

(KURT thinks for a moment)

KURT
Helga.

ANTON
What?

KURT
That's your name now. Helga.

ANTON
No.

KURT
What's wrong with Helga? It's a good Bavarian
name.

ANTON
It's a woman's name.

KURT
I thought you didn't know many names.

ANTON
Don't mock me.

KURT
Well then what about Ingrid? Or Eva? Or...

ANTON
Do not mock me!

KURT
Then pick a name, dammit!

(Beat)

ANTON
You raised your voice to me.

KURT
You raised yours first.

ANTON
Aren't you afraid of me?

KURT
I am. But I'm also in my cups. Means I can do
stupid things even when I'm scared.

*(For the first time, ANTON smiles, almost chuck-
ling)*

ANTON
You are a strange man.

KURT
Oh? What does that make you then?

ANTON
Just...strange.

(Beat)

ANTON
Anton.

KURT
What's that?

ANTON
You can call me Anton. Like your saint.

KURT
Anton it is, then. I'm Kurt Volker.

(KURT offers his hand. ANTON shakes it. KURT winces at his grip)

KURT
Good Christ!

ANTON
Did I hurt you?

KURT
Yes! That's my drinking hand, too!

ANTON
I am sorry. I did not mean to...

KURT
It's all right. Give me a moment.

(KURT wrings his hand out)

KURT
You're quite the ox, huh?

ANTON
I'm strong, if that's what you mean.

KURT
Good for you. The world always needs strong men.

(He pours some booze in a glass and offers it to ANTON)

KURT
It'll keep you warm.

(ANTON drinks, KURT sits)

KURT
So what brings you to my boneyard, Anton the ox?

(ANTON doesn't respond)

KURT
Most folks don't find themselves here acciden-tally. They're either mourners or...well, the ones being mourned.

ANTON
I was drawn here.

KURT
Really?

ANTON
This place is familiar to me.

KURT
So you've been here before.

ANTON
Perhaps.

KURT
Did I put one of yours in the ground here? Your
mother? Your father?

ANTON
Why do you limp?

(Beat)

KURT
Beg pardon?

ANTON
You walk with a limp. I want to know why.

KURT
Don't see how that's any...

ANTON
Are you damaged?

KURT
I don't want to talk about it!

ANTON
I'm only asking...

KURT
And I'm telling you, leave it alone. Just because I
took pity on you doesn't mean I want to tell you
my Goddamn life story. *(Beat)* Do you have any
family hereabouts? Someone to take you in?

ANTON
I have a father. But he won't claim me.

KURT
So you're a bastard then?

ANTON
I've been called that.

KURT
You and me both. *(Drinks)* Well, it's not a palace, but you can sleep here tonight if you want. At least you'll be dry. Then you can...go wherever you're going.

ANTON
I'm not going anywhere. I was trying to die.

KURT
Well, you can't do it here. I won't let you.

ANTON
If I decided to, you couldn't stop me.

KURT
Oh! You're a tough one, then.

ANTON
You know I am.

(KURT puts his arm on the table, ready to arm wrestle)

ANTON
What?

KURT
Put your arm up here and show me.

ANTON
I don't understand.

KURT
You've never done this before?

ANTON
I don't know.

KURT
All right, all right. Put your arm up here, like

mine.

(ANTON does so. KURT grabs his hand)

KURT
Now, you try to push my arm down, and I'll try to push yours down. Whoever does it, wins.

ANTON
This is childish.

KURT
Let's see how strong you are when I know what's coming.

ANTON
I don't see...

KURT
Don't let my limp fool you. I've got muscles that...

(ANTON slams KURT's arm down with ease. He's so forceful that KURT falls out of his chair)

KURT
Jesus Christ!

ANTON
I win.

KURT
I wasn't ready yet, dammit!

ANTON
Yes. But I won.

KURT
Again! We're going again.

(He puts his arm up. ANTON grabs it)

KURT
Now this time, don't move til I say so. On the
count of three. One...

*(KURT immediately starts to push, hoping to trick
ANTON. ANTON's arm doesn't move)*

KURT
...move, dammit...

ANTON
Are we going again?

KURT
...come on....come on...

*(ANTON slams KURT's arm down again, knock-
ing him out of his chair. KURT lies there, stunned)*

ANTON
I win again.

KURT
Sweet merciful Jesus. I've never seen anything
like that.

ANTON
Shall we go again?

KURT
No, no. If there's one thing life's taught me over
and over again, it's to know when I'm beat. *(Rises,
dusting himself off)* You're with the circus, aren't
you?

ANTON
What?

KURT
A strongman or something? Pulling nails out of
boards with your bare teeth? Bending iron bars

in two?

KURT
ANTON
I've never even seen a circus.

KURT
You should seek one out. They'd welcome you, no doubt.

ANTON
I do not do well in the company of others.

KURT
We're getting along fine.

ANTON
Hmm.

KURT
Is it your face? Trust me, a circus wouldn't care about that. They might love it, in fact.

ANTON
I don't like being stared at.

KURT
You might want to unwrap yourself then. Draws a lot of attention.

ANTON
I would draw even more attention without the bandages.

KURT
Can't be that bad.

ANTON
It's that bad and worse.

KURT
Do you mind if I ask?

ANTON
Ask what?

KURT
About your face. Was it an accident? I know a man, worked at the University. Knocked over a beaker of acid. Damn near melted his left side.

ANTON
It wasn't acid.

KURT
Poor fellow looked like an old candle.

ANTON
I do not wish to discuss it.

KURT
I'm just asking.

(Beat)

ANTON
I will tell you about my face when you tell me about your limp.

(Beat)

KURT
Fair enough. *(Rises)* Well, Anton the Ox, I'm off to bed. It's the only one I got, but...

(He looks into another room offstage)

KURT
I've got the side room there, where I keep my tools. There's some hay-bales that'll serve for a bed. It's yours if you want it.

ANTON
I should leave.

KURT
And go where?

ANTON
You should not take me in.

KURT
Well, I already have, so...

ANTON
Wherever I go, tragedy follows.

KURT
Tragedy and I know each other very well. I don't fear it, and neither should you.

(ANTON stands there, unmoving. The room fills with the sound of thunder and a flash of lightning)

KURT
Besides, the downpour's still going strong.

(ANTON says nothing)

KURT
Ah, do what you will. I'd tell you not to steal anything, but I've got nothing worth taking.

(KURT heads off, stopping at the doorway. He stares at ANTON for a bit, clearly waiting for him to say something. Finally--)

KURT
You're welcome.

(ANTON doesn't respond. KURT sighs and goes to bed. ANTON stays at the window, watching the lightning. Finally, he goes to to the door and leaves the shack. Lights change)

SCENE FOUR

(The graveyard, the same night. A fog hangs in the air. NADYA is at a grave, throwing things into a sack. She carries a small, dim lantern. ANTON approaches silently)

ANTON
What are you doing?

(Startled, she spins around, drawing a knife)

NADYA
Stay back.

ANTON
What are you doing here?

NADYA
Another step, and I'll slit your throat for you.

(He steps close enough that she can see him better. She's taken aback at his size)

NADYA
Good God.

ANTON
Put your knife down.

NADYA
I think I'll keep it where it is.

ANTON
Put it down or I'll break your arm, woman.

(Beat. She sheathes the blade)

NADYA
Don't touch me.

ANTON
I won't.

NADYA
Good.

(She grabs her bag, backing away)

NADYA
I didn't hear you come up on me.

ANTON
I didn't wish to be heard, so I wasn't.

NADYA
Simple as that?

ANTON
That was all the thought I put into it.

NADYA
Neamt Jegos.

ANTON
What?

NADYA
What?

ANTON
I don't know what you said.

(Beat)

NADYA
It loses something in translation.

ANTON
What are you doing here?

NADYA
I could ask you the same question.

ANTON
I could break your neck and take that sack from you.

NADYA
Doamne! Not one for social graces, are you?

ANTON
No.

NADYA
How does this sound? Why don't I just leave the graveyard, and you go back to wherever you came from?

ANTON
No.

NADYA
You're the gravedigger. Is that it? A loyal dog guarding his hole?

ANTON
I am...Anton.Yes.

NADYA
Are you certain?

ANTON
I am only recently named. It does not sound like
my own yet.

(Beat)

NADYA
I don't know what that means.

ANTON
I don't know how else to explain it.

(She smiles. He stares at her for a bit)

ANTON
I like the way you smile.

NADYA
Yes?

ANTON
Your face is lovely.

NADYA
So I've been told.

ANTON
What is your name?

NADYA
Nadya.

ANTON
Nad-ya...

NADYA
That's it.

ANTON
What is in your bag, Nadya?

(Beat)

NADYA
Bones.

ANTON
Why do you have a bag of bones?

NADYA
Why do you think?

ANTON
I have no idea. That's why I asked.

NADYA
I'm Romani.

(ANTON pauses, trying to place the word)

ANTON
A gypsy.

NADYA
That's right. And I use these...

(She shakes the bag)

NADYA
...to see the future.

ANTON
You're lying.

NADYA
Don't call me a liar.

ANTON
No one can see the future.

NADYA
I have a long list of clienti who'd say otherwise.

ANTON
I do not believe in superstition.

NADYA
Then what?

ANTON
Science. I believe in science.

NADYA
Are they so different?

(She sits down. He stares at her)

NADYA
Well, if we're going to have a chat, sit down
already.

ANTON
The ground is wet from the rain.

(She immediately stands up, examining her dress)

NADYA
Dammit! Soaked right through.

(ANTON smiles, laughs a little)

NADYA
That's funny to you?

ANTON
Yes. Your bottom is wet.

NADYA
Thank you, I'm well aware.

(He starts to laugh more)

NADYA
Yes, yes. Please, remain amused.

ANTON
You knew that it had rained, and you sat down
anyway. That was foolish.

NADYA
I wasn't thinking.

ANTON
You behaved foolishly.

NADYA
Are you quite finished?

ANTON
And now your bottom is wet.

(His laughter peters out naturally. He just smiles)

NADYA
You're a strange giant.

ANTON
I haven't laughed before. At least...not that I remember.

NADYA
Nonsense.

ANTON
It's true. I am younger than I look.

NADYA
I cannot tell how you look at all, wrapped as you are.

(She reaches for his bandages. He backs away)

ANTON
No.

NADYA
Am I so terrifying?

ANTON
Do not touch me.

NADYA
Hmm. Not something I am often told.

ANTON
Why would you want to...?

NADYA
See your face? I am always curious. The more
something is hidden, the more I want to take it
out of the shadows.

ANTON
I belong where no one can see me.

NADYA
That only makes me...oh!

*(She pretends to trip. ANTON instinctually catches
her. She holds onto him)*

NADYA
And look. We're touching. Not so bad, is it?

*(ANTON feels conflicting emotions, but does not
release her)*

ANTON
Don't.

NADYA
Don't what?

ANTON
My face...do not touch it.

NADYA
I haven't, and I won't.

ANTON
But before...you tried to see it and...

NADYA
I will see it when you let me, not before.

ANTON
I will never want that.

NADYA
Oh, I can be very persuasive.

(She jumps out of his arms)

NADYA
Well, since I've provided the evening's entertain-
ment, perhaps you'll let me leave with this bag
and with my limbs intact.

ANTON
I will not hurt you.

NADYA
I wouldn't have let you if you tried.

ANTON
I don't want you to leave.

NADYA
That's sweet, but I'm not staying in a graveyard all
night. Lots of strigoi about.

(Beat)

NADYA
Evil spirits.

ANTON
You like to use words that I don't know. It makes
you feel smart.

NADYA
You're a clever maimuță.

(She starts to leave)

NADYA
I'll see you next time, Anton.

ANTON
You will return?

NADYA
Yes. I think I will.

ANTON
Then...are we friends?

(She smiles)

NADYA
Stranger things have happened.

(She exits. Lights change)

Scene Five

(KURT's shack, the next morning. KURT staggers about the room, hung over. He splashes some cold water on his face)

KURT
Ah! Dammit!

(He shakes it off, and goes to ANTON's room. No one is there)

KURT
Back to the circus with you then.

(He grabs a shovel for the day's work. He goes to the door and opens it. ANTON is standing there. KURT jumps back, startled)

KURT
This is not the ideal face to wake to.

ANTON
I want to stay.

KURT
What?

(ANTON mistakes the question for not hearing him. He speaks unnecessarily loud)

ANTON
I WANT TO STAY!

KURT
I heard you, you damn lummox! I just...get inside already!

(ANTON enters)

ANTON
If your offer still stands, I would like to stay here with you.

KURT
My...what the hell?

ANTON
You offered me the tool room.

KURT
For one damn night!

ANTON
I wish to stay longer.

KURT
Well, I wish for a buxom lady with a stein between her breasts. Mine is a life of disappointment.

(ANTON just stares at him)

KURT
And now I remember that you don't understand jokes.

ANTON
A gypsy sat on wet dirt and got her bottom wet.

(Beat)

KURT
I don't get it.

ANTON
It was a joke.

KURT
I still don't get it.

ANTON
It made me laugh.

(KURT rubs his eyes in frustration)

KURT
So you want to stay.

ANTON
Yes.

KURT
Why?

(Beat)

ANTON
I have nowhere else to go. I came here to die, but I
no longer wish that. And I like it here.

KURT
You like the graveyard?

ANTON
It's peaceful. I've known very little peace in my life.

KURT
I like the quiet myself.

ANTON
So I can stay?

KURT
Give me a damn minute, will you? I'm barely
awake and....

(KURT sits down. ANTON joins him)

KURT
You have no money, no prospects, and I should
just...what? Give up my peace and quiet for a
boarder? I don't even know you.

ANTON
I don't know you either.

KURT
That's hardly the point, is it?

ANTON
Is it?

KURT
Jesus, every time you open your mouth, I don't
know whether to laugh or punch you!

ANTON
You helped me before. Why won't you help me now?

KURT
Not that simple.

ANTON
Explain it to me.

KURT
I can't.

ANTON
I want to understand.

KURT
Stop talking! Just...can you shut your flapping jaws for a trice?

(Beat. KURT composes himself)

KURT
I've been alone here for a while now. That's the way I prefer it. When other people are around... they complicate things. I don't like complication.

ANTON
I am a complication?

KURT
Yes. I'm sorry, but yes.

ANTON
And so you do not like me?

KURT
I didn't say that. You're all right, I guess. You either talk too much or too little, but...yes, I've known worse than you.

ANTON
Thank you.

KURT
I just... I'm a drunken, crippled ass. I'm not a good companion.

ANTON
I like you.

KURT
Why?

ANTON
Because you have been kinder to me than anyone has been in my entire life.

KURT
I'm sorry to hear that.

(KURT thinks for a bit)

KURT
I'll tell you a secret.

ANTON
All right.

KURT
I'm a hair's breadth from losing this job.

ANTON
Really?

KURT
I can't dig for shit anymore. I have a hard enough time getting around with this...

(He taps his brace)

KURT
And the church...they keep me on as a kindness, but there's no way I can keep up. People drop like flies in this town. They can't afford to hire another man to help, so...there it is.

ANTON
I could dig for you.

KURT
Yes. You could.

ANTON
I'm stronger than anyone. I can dig many graves.

KURT
At night. You dig at night, stay in this shack during the day. That way no one will know.

ANTON
That works well for me. I have no desire to draw
attention to myself.

KURT
I won't be able to pay you, but you can stay here
and share your meals with me.

ANTON
That is all I ask.

KURT
All right then.

ANTON
You are helping me again.

KURT
No. I'm helping myself. You just happen to be
here.

ANTON
I think it's more than that.

KURT
It's not.

ANTON
I think it is.

KURT
Shut your gob before I change my mind, lummox.

ANTON
Thank you.

KURT
And don't thank me! This is entirely self-serving.

ANTON
You are a good man.

KURT
And you're one sentence away from fouling the deal.

(ANTON offers his hand)

KURT
Gentle this time. I like my knuckles lined up the way they are.

ANTON
All right.

(They shake. ANTON doesn't hurt him)

KURT
All right.

(Lights fade)

SCENE SIX

(That night, the cemetery. ANTON is rising out of the hole, shovel in hand. KURT is watching him)

KURT
That was a hell of a thing.

ANTON
This is large enough for a casket, yes?

KURT
That's large enough for a fat burgomeister and half his fat family.

ANTON
Then you are satisfied?

KURT
Stunned is more like it. But...yes, well done.

ANTON
Good.

KURT
That took you...

(He checks his pocket watch)

KURT
...not even an hour. And I don't see a drop of sweat.

ANTON
It was not difficult work.

KURT
How can you say that? In my prime, that hole would've taken me half the night.

ANTON
Your prime and mine are two different things.

KURT
And that's God's truth. *(offers ANTON his bottle)* You may not need it, but you earned it.

(ANTON takes the bottle and drains it)

KURT
Hey! Not the whole thing!

ANTON
Oh. I'm sorry.

(KURT takes out another and drinks)

KURT
Ah, no harm done.

ANTON
It's good. This...what is it?

KURT
Schnapps.

ANTON
I like it.

KURT
If there's one thing we Bavarians know, it's
schnapps.

(They sit by the hole, drinking)

KURT
Where are you from, Anton?

ANTON
Many places, I suppose. I think I was born in
Ingolstadt, but...most of my life was spent in
Switzerland.

KURT
An orphan?

ANTON
Abandoned. My father saw my face and left me.

KURT
Christ, I'm sorry to hear that.

ANTON
I hate him. Or...I hated him. I can no longer tell
the difference.

KURT
You must've done well enough. Got an education.

ANTON
Only experience. Little of it good.

KURT
You speak proper.

ANTON
I enjoy language. For a time, I could barely

communicate. It was maddening...to have these thoughts and these feelings...to have the urge to express them, but no ability to do so.

KURT
For some people, that would be an improvement.

ANTON
It is a hard thing. I imagine all who live wish to be understood.

KURT
Anton, my friend, I will drink to that. *(KURT drinks)*

ANTON
I've never had a friend.

KURT
Come now.

ANTON
Truly. Those who did not wish me dead simply ran from me.

KURT
You're a hunted man, then?

ANTON
Once. But I've fled beyond their reach.

KURT
A criminal?

ANTON
I've done...terrible things. I was very young and had no control over what I felt. I raged against those who hurt me most, and some died because of it.

(KURT makes the sign of the cross over ANTON and splashes his face with alcohol)

KURT
Ego te absolvo.

ANTON
I am wet. And confused.

KURT
I just absolved you of your sins. And I did it in Latin.

ANTON
You did?

KURT
Oh yes. It's the language God likes his prayers in.

ANTON
Are you a priest?

(KURT drinks, then rises)

KURT
Well, Brother Anton. I'm off to perform a miracle: Turning schnapps into piss. If that's not a sign of the Lord's existence, I don't know what is.

ANTON
What should I do?

KURT
Whatever you'd like. This is your home now.

ANTON
I need...guidance.

(KURT puts a hand on ANTON's shoulder)

KURT
You know what I do when I'm in need of thinking?

ANTON
No. How could I know that?

KURT
I walk amongst the graves. I read what little I can on the stones, learn of the people this earth holds. I suggest you take your past, and bury it in one of these plots. And then, start thinking about your future.

ANTON
I've never thought of the future. Only where I was, and what I felt at the moment.

KURT
Pfft. A fine way to achieve nothing. You want to find happiness, lummox? Decide what you want your life to be, then make it that.

ANTON
Is that how you ended up a gravedigger?

(Beat. KURT chuckles)

KURT
That's a story for another time.

(He exits. Lights fade)

Scene Seven

(A month later. ANTON has found better clothes, though his face is still bandaged. NADYA pokes her head up out of the burial hole. ANTON stands above her, offering her his hand. She lets out a startled cry, then laughs)

NADYA
Hello, giant.

ANTON
Hello, Nadya.

(She takes his hand. He lifts her out of the hole with great ease, almost hurling her. She staggers but catches herself)

ANTON
Oh! I'm sorry.

NADYA
Christos! If I was meant to fly, I'd have a beak and feathers.

ANTON
Chickens have beaks and feathers, but they do
not fly.

NADYA
Yes they do.

ANTON
I do not think so.

NADYA
Chickens fly, Anton.

ANTON
I've never seen them do so.

(She laughs)

NADYA
I have seen many strange men in my day, but you
may well be the strangest.

ANTON
You do not need to insult me.

NADYA
Not an insult. Strange means interesting. Very,
very, VERY few men are interesting anymore.

ANTON
Oh. Thank you.

NADYA
Bentru Putin.

ANTON
Did you come for more bones?

NADYA
Not this time.

(She tosses him a bag. He looks into it)

ANTON
You have a bag of dirt.

NADYA
Grave dirt. Very potent.

ANTON
How can dirt be potent?

NADYA
Good for seeing the past or the future.

(He just stares at her)

NADYA
I have a new client. Wants to see his future. I
asked him some questions, and he mentioned
this graveyard several times. So I'll take the dirt,
mix it with some wax and make a candle.

ANTON
To see his future?

NADYA
Yes.

ANTON
With a candle?

NADYA
Yes.

(Beat)

ANTON
You are just as strange as I am.

NADYA
What I am is penniless. I'll take whatever clientii
I can get. So, this last month has been good to
you, yes?

ANTON
What?

NADYA
You're looking less...ragged.

ANTON
I do not understand.

NADYA
Those clothes. Better than the scraps you were wearing before.

ANTON
I took them off a dead man.

NADYA
Ha! Well, he did not need them anymore.

ANTON
My thought as well.

NADYA
We have something in common. We are both of us corbi, picking off the dead.

ANTON
You mean crows.

NADYA
Very good, giant! You've learned some of my language.

ANTON
I was hoping to see you again.

NADYA
And you were hoping to impress me, yes?

(Beat)

ANTON
I would ask a favor of you.

NADYA
Oh yes? What might that be?

ANTON
I want to know my future.

NADYA
Ah. Is that all?

ANTON
Should I ask for more?

NADYA
You should always ask for what you want. And be prepared not to get it.

ANTON
My life has taught me to expect nothing from anyone.

NADYA
And yet here you stand, with a set of new clothes.

(Beat)

ANTON
You make a good point.

NADYA
So what of your future do you wish to know?

ANTON
Anything. Everything.

NADYA
Those are two very different answers.

ANTON
I have never thought of my future. In fact, I
doubted I would ever live this long. But now...

NADYA
Your life has changed.

ANTON
Yes.

NADYA
For the better?

ANTON
I think so. I hope so.

NADYA
And you wish to know if this better life will last.

ANTON
Very much.

NADYA
Sit with me.

(She takes him by the hand and they sit)

NADYA
Why do you hide your face?

ANTON
I have no face.

NADYA
You have eyes. Two different colors.

ANTON
It is how I was made.

NADYA
And a mouth. And I'm guessing a nose.

ANTON
Yes. But together they are...monstrous.

NADYA
I'm sorry.

ANTON
I have always looked this way. This graveyard is
the first place where people have not fled from
me.

NADYA
It's why I like places like this. A sanctuary for
outcasts.

(She notices him staring at her)

NADYA
I am so lovely you cannot help but stare? Is that it?

ANTON
You do not seem like an outcast.

NADYA
I am a gypsy. We belong nowhere.

ANTON
You have tribes. Your friends and family who...

NADYA
I am the last of my people here. The others have
moved on.

ANTON
And you did not go with them?

NADYA
I couldn't. They cast me out.

ANTON
Why?

NADYA
It hurts to tell it.

ANTON
I understand.

NADYA
You couldn't. It didn't happen to you.

ANTON
My own life...what little I had, I have lost. I carry
that loss with me everywhere I go.

(She stares at him)

NADYA
Is that where your kindness comes from?

ANTON
Am I kind?

NADYA
Very. You have a child's heart. It gives itself
completely, and shatters at the smallest hurt.

ANTON
I wish I was stronger. Inside.

NADYA
You will be strong, or you will be dead. The world
welcomes no others.

ANTON
It is that cruel?

NADYA
That cruel and worse.

(Beat)

NADYA
I had a child.

ANTON
You seem too young.

NADYA
Not so young as all that. My child...my girl...she
was încrucişat...

(She struggles to translate the word)

NADYA
Mixed. Her father was not of my tribe. Not of
any tribe.

ANTON
That is why they sent you away?

NADYA
Yes. With my people, that is a great shame. It does
not wash off. They cast me to the winds.

ANTON
I'm sorry.

NADYA
I was young. A fool. I went to the father...a man
of numbers. A...what is a man who counts money?

ANTON
A banker?

NADYA
Banker, yes. He had come to my camp, and I had
loved him. But I loved him with a child's love...
foolish. I came to his house, and his wife answered.

ANTON
He was married to another?

NADYA
As I said...I was a fool. He came to the door,
dragged me to the field and threw us to the

ground. Me and my Dorina.

ANTON
I don't know that word.

NADYA
Not a word; a name. It means "gift." My gift. Her father wanted nothing to do with us, swore to kill us if he saw us again. So I ran. Tried to live in the wood, but...

(Beat)

NADYA
Dorina did not survive a year.

(ANTON struggles to reign in his emotions)

NADYA
I see your rage, Anton. But this is the past, and cannot be changed.

ANTON
I want to hurt this man.

NADYA
As did I. But it would help nothing. Murder does not bring peace.

(She looks in his eyes)

NADYA
You know this better than most.

ANTON
I do.

NADYA
And so I came here. Ingolstadt is a good enough place. Lots of places to hide. Lots of drunks who don't guard their pockets.

ANTON
You are a thief?

NADYA
I am whatever I need to be to survive.

ANTON
I understand that.

(He realizes they're still holding hands)

ANTON
You have my hand.

NADYA
I've been reading it.

ANTON
What?

NADYA
Your hands hold many things, including the future. I've been following their lines, trying to learn where they lead.

ANTON
Oh. I...should I pay you?

NADYA
You have let me steal bones and dirt. And eased my burden a little. No charge, this time.

ANTON
What do you see?

NADYA
It is...confusing. Yours is a strange hand.

ANTON
It is?

NADYA
You are...were a man of the fields. A farmer.

ANTON
No.

NADYA
You were. I can see it.

ANTON
I have never spent a day in the fields.

NADYA
You are certain?

ANTON
I am.

(She stares at him, confused, then tries to read on. She smiles)

NADYA
You have known great love.

ANTON
I have?

NADYA
I see it here. A wife that you loved above all others.

ANTON
No.

(She stares at him, frustrated)

NADYA
I know what is on your palm, Anton.

ANTON
Whatever you are reading there...that life didn't belong to me.

NADYA
I think you are being stubborn.

ANTON
I think you are perhaps not as good at this as you think.

(She gasps in mock outrage, smacks his arm)

NADYA
You would say such things to one you fancy?

ANTON
You think I fancy you because of what you see in my palm?

NADYA
Because of what I see in your eyes. And I do not "think". I know.

(He is embarrassed by this)

NADYA
There is no shame in this, my giant. Few can resist my charms.

ANTON
You are very confident.

NADYA
(shrugging) I am many things, all of which are Nadya. *(She can see he is embarrassed)* Do not look away. What you feel is a good thing. The rush of blood, the blush of the cheek...nothing is better.

ANTON
I do not want to discuss it.

NADYA
So bashful, you are.

ANTON
It makes me feel strange. Weak. Confused.

NADYA
It is the way of affection. But it should be
embraced, not feared.

ANTON
But what if the...what if it is not returned?

(Beat. NADYA smiles, understanding)

NADYA
My sweet, kind-hearted friend...why do you
think so little of yourself?

(He pulls his hand away)

ANTON
I am a monster.

NADYA
Not in my eyes.

ANTON
You would not say that if you knew the things
I've done. The people I've hurt...killed...

NADYA
A monster would not hurt inside as you do
now.

ANTON
I do not know how to atone for them.

NADYA
You can't. You can only do what you have already
done.

ANTON
Start over.

NADYA
Yes. Give me your other hand.

ANTON
What?

NADYA
This hand tells me your past. It is your future you
wish to see, yes?

ANTON
I do.

NADYA
Then my friend, give me your other hand.

*(He gives it to her. She stares at it for a moment,
then leaps up & backs away)*

NADYA
Cacat!

ANTON
What is it?

NADYA
What are you?!

ANTON
I do not understand.

NADYA
Why do you have two hands?

ANTON
Is that...most people have two of them.

NADYA
Not...

*(She grabs his hands, holding them up to inspect
them)*

NADYA
These are not the same hands! Nothing about them is the same!

ANTON
Each has four fingers and a thumb.

NADYA
They do not even feel the same! The palm, the knuckles...even the skin...you have the hands of two different people.

(ANTON pulls his hands away, his anger rising)

NADYA
Is your face like this? A collection of other men's faces?

ANTON
Do not ask me that.

NADYA
Good God, what are you?

ANTON
I told you before. I am a monster.

NADYA
I didn't believe you.

ANTON
Do you now?

(She backs away, her hand on her knife)

NADYA
Don't hurt me.

ANTON
Why do you...?

(She draws her knife)

NADYA
Don't!

ANTON
I am not your enemy!

NADYA
I'm going to leave now, Anton.

ANTON
No!

NADYA
I am going to leave, and you are going to stay. Do you understand me?

ANTON
Please. You are my friend.

(She is about to respond, but thinks better of it. She sheathes her knife)

NADYA
Just let me go.

ANTON
Do not hate me, Nadya. I could not bear it.

(He goes to her. She backs away)

ANTON
You were going to tell me my future. Please, just sit. We can talk and...

NADYA
You have no future, giant. None at all.

ANTON
Nadya...!

(She runs off. ANTON stands there, a storm of anger and sorrow. In his rage, he rips a headstone from the ground. Lights fade)

SCENE EIGHT

(That same night, but several hours later. It is almost dawn. A table is set in the corner of the stage, with a cloth cover and a small bowl of water. NADYA enters with a hand-made candle. She lights it, lets the flame grow)

NADYA
You can come in.

(VICTOR enters. He is a changed man, much more haggard than in Scene 1)

NADYA
Sit.

(He sits at the table)

VICTOR
I appreciate your expediency.

NADYA
I appreciate your gold. Good motivation to get this done tonight.

VICTOR
Did it take you long? To make the candle?

(She fans the flame)

NADYA
You don't believe in this, do you?

VICTOR
It's up to you to make a believer out of me.

NADYA
Give the fire a moment to do its job.

(She sits down)

NADYA
Dawn is a good time to tell the future, just as a new day is born.

VICTOR
What is this ceromancy supposed to tell me?

NADYA
That is a doctor's word for seeing in wax, yes?

VICTOR
Yes.

NADYA
I like you, domnule. We both use strange words to confuse those around us.

VICTOR
I did not pay for banter.

NADYA
I am to see in the wax, yes? Hard to do until the candle melts some.

(She leans over the table, showing her cleavage)

NADYA
There are other things we can do to pass the time.

VICTOR
No.

NADYA
I promise you, I am worth the price.

(She reaches to touch his face. He grabs her wrist tightly)

VICTOR
The only woman I ever loved had her neck snapped like dry wood. Don't touch me again.

NADYA
I do not like threats so much.

(VICTOR rises, crosses to her)

VICTOR
Do not mistake me for some common alley-rat you can gut and leave in the snow. I am a baron, a doctor and in no way a man to be trifled with.

(She rises, meeting his gaze)

NADYA
Then why come to me?

VICTOR
Because all sane means of finding my quarry have failed, so I must resort to...this.

(They stare at each other for a bit. She then laughs)

NADYA
Desperation can be a good thing, boierule. It can be the best thing.

(She motions for him to sit. He does so. She takes the candle and holds it above the bowl, carefully letting a small amount of wax drip into it)

VICTOR
What do you see?

NADYA
Give me a moment. This is an art, not a science.

VICTOR
Do not bait me, woman. I...

NADYA
Who do you seek? Tell me of him.

VICTOR
What?

NADYA
Speak while the wax forms! The more I know, the clearer I will see.

VICTOR
He is large...very tall and broad.

NADYA
Good.

VICTOR
He burned through my life like a wildfire. Murdered my brother, my friends, my father... my wife.

NADYA
Yes. I can see it. He is close.

VICTOR
How close?!

NADYA
Very. You have tracked him to Ingolstadt, yes?

VICTOR
Yes. I was a student here. It was where we were first...acquainted. I thought perhaps he would return and...

NADYA
He has but...wait....

(She drips more wax into the bowl. She starts at what she sees within)

NADYA
You must stop this hunt.

VICTOR
What did you see?

NADYA
There is a chain wrapped tight around the two of you. If you continue to hunt him, it will be death for you both.

VICTOR
I don't care! If my death brings his about, then it will be worth it.

NADYA
You speak madness. Stop, and rebuild a life. If you leave this place, you and your prey will never see each other again.

VICTOR
I can't. He's more than my prey. Any lives he takes will fall squarely on my head.

NADYA
I don't understand.

VICTOR
I made him.

NADYA
This man is your son?

VICTOR
He is no man. He's a monster. Scarred and malformed...he...

(She backs away. VICTOR sees the recognition in her eyes)

VICTOR
You've seen him.

NADYA
No.

(He grabs her roughly. She doesn't fight back)

VICTOR
Where is he?!

NADYA
Let me go!

VICTOR
You have no gypsy camp to come to your rescue, woman. Tell me where he is!

NADYA
I saw death in the water! If you chase him any longer, you will meet your end in a land of snow and frozen seas!

VICTOR
I don't give a damn for your prophecies. Just tell me where he is!

(He takes a knife and holds it to her)

NADYA
Kill me and you'll never find him.

VICTOR
There are other gypsies besides you. I imagine
my coin will make them forthcoming.

(She is about to speak, but stops)

VICTOR
Ah. Is that it?

*(He opens a belt-pouch, and produces several gold
coins. She reaches for them, and he drops them on
the floor. She scrambles to pick them up. A moment
of shame takes VICTOR)*

VICTOR
I should be a better man than this.

NADYA
So say all dogs.

VICTOR
But for one mistake, my life would have been
full of light. A family, a noble title, and scientific
advancement. Now...

NADYA
Yes. All eyes weep for you, rich man.

VICTOR
I would gladly part with every franc if it would
put an end to this nightmare.

*(She rises, clutching the coins. He reads her expres-
sion)*

VICTOR
Yours has been a hard life, I take it.

(She spits on the ground)

NADYA
That is what I think of your pity.

VICTOR
Then what do you think of this?

(He removes his coin pouch, holds it)

VICTOR
There is enough here for you to start over. The dream of every pauper. And all you have to do is tell me where to find the monster.

NADYA
So that you can kill him?

VICTOR
I'm not killing him. I'm taking back a life I should never have given.

(Beat)

VICTOR
This is not your story. Take these coins, and remove yourself from it.

(A long beat. She reaches out. He puts the coin pouch in her hand)

NADYA
Sit. We have much to discuss.

(They sit. She blows out the candle. Blackout)

END OF ACT ONE

ACT II

Scene One

(Lights up. KURT's shack. It is a mess. ANTON is huddled in a corner. KURT enters, carrying a small barrel)

KURT
Stop your worrying, lummox. I have returned with beer and...

(He sees the wreck of his room)

KURT
Christ almighty...

(He sees ANTON)

KURT
Anton! Are you hurt? Anton!

(ANTON rises. His chest is bleeding, & he holds a bloody knife)

ANTON
...Kurt...

KURT
Oh God, boy. You hold still. I have bandages and...

ANTON
...why won't I die?

KURT
Don't you worry. You're not dying, not so long as
I'm here.

ANTON
This knife...I buried it deep...no man could have
survived...

KURT
What?

ANTON
A man can die. A man should die. But I am not a
man.

(KURT has found a cloth, tries to press it to
ANTON's chest. ANTON holds his knife up and
KURT stops)

ANTON
I thrust it all the way into my heart. Through the
muscle, between the ribs...I felt the blade touch
my backbone...I saw my blood pour out of the
hole.

KURT
That's impossible.

ANTON
But my heart did not stop beating. The pain didn't
leave me. I live and...

(In a sudden rage, ANTON thrusts knife into the
table)

ANTON
I should not live! I never should have lived, but
here I am, a mockery of nature and...

(ANTON grabs KURT by the shoulders)

ANTON
The night we met...I had come to this cemetery
to die. Can you help me? Will you help me?

KURT
Help you what?

ANTON
Die! I want to die, I...

(He starts pounding on his bloody chest)

ANTON
I cannot take the pain! Everything I feel turns on
me, and then...Kurt, you are my only friend. If you
do not kill me...

KURT
I won't!

ANTON
...then I will kill you.

(Beat)

ANTON
I do not wish to. But already, I can feel murder
rising up inside me. Soon, I will go mad and when
that happens...

(He grabs some rope)

ANTON
This. Take this. Strangle me. If my breath stops, my
heart might follow.

KURT
No.

ANTON
Please! I'm begging you!

KURT
Listen to me. I have broken damn near every
vow I've ever taken, but I will never kill a man.
Certainly not you.

(ANTON falls to his knees, weeping)

ANTON
...please...I want the pain to stop...

(KURT kneels next to him)

KURT
It doesn't. I know that better than anyone. But life
isn't about the absence of pain. It's about endur-
ing it.

ANTON
I cannot. I love, I find peace, and every time
it is taken from me. And when it is...I've felt
a neck break in my hands. I don't want it to be
your neck.

KURT
Nor do I.

ANTON
You should fear me. You should fear what I can do.

KURT
Don't tell me what to do, lummox.

*(KURT smiles. ANTON's mood softens. KURT
puts his arm around him)*

KURT
Whatever happened to you while I was in town...
for God's sake, you don't have to kill yourself over
it.

ANTON
She was my friend. She was kind to me. Then she
saw what I am, what I truly am, and she fled.

(There is a long silence between them)

KURT
A woman. I should have known.

(ANTON just stares at him)

KURT
You're not the first to go mad over a broken heart,
Anton. Nor will you be the last.

ANTON
All my life, I have been betrayed. Always.

KURT
"Always?" No such thing. A child is always a child
until it becomes a boy, then a man, then a corpse.
Trust an old gravedigger on that.

ANTON
She said I had no future.

KURT
Pfft! Will you wake up tomorrow? Will you do
something then? That's the future. Happens
whether we think it will or not.

(KURT pats ANTON on the chest, then winces)

KURT
Oh God, I'm sorry.

ANTON
Why?

KURT
Didn't that hurt? Where you cut yourself?

ANTON
No. And I didn't cut myself. I stabbed myself.

KURT
I'd think you were drunk if I hadn't drained the
last drop yesterday.

ANTON
You don't believe me?

KURT
Well...when you love a woman and then...I think
you're not thinking straight is all.

ANTON
Do you know much about women?

KURT
Yes! Or...perhaps not as much as some, but...what
kind of question is that?

ANTON
I don't know. How many kinds of questions are
there?

*(Beat. KURT starts to laugh. ANTON smiles. As
the laughter peters out--)*

KURT
You were right about me.

(ANTON stares at him)

KURT
I was a priest. Long ago. A lifetime ago. I was

happier then...until I met a woman.

ANTON
Had you not met women before?

KURT
No, I...this woman in particular.

ANTON
Oh.

KURT
A married woman at that. The Father had hired
her to clean the church and...she wasn't a great
beauty, Anton. But her heart...kind, and pure,
and nothing but love for this whole rotten world.
We would talk, and she would laugh and...God,
that laugh. Hers was a marriage of convenience,
though not damn convenient for me. I loved her.
I didn't want to, I tried not to, but it happened
all the same.

ANTON
Did she love you in return?

KURT
She did. And so I abandoned everything I believed
in, the life I thought would be my fate forever, all
for her.

ANTON
What of her husband?

KURT
We kept it a secret at first. Her from him, me from
the church. But secrets never keep, so I left the
clergy. She left her husband too, but...

(Beat. He takes a drink)

KURT
He killed her, Anton. Took a knife and just...
and then he came for me. I was in the church,
saying my goodbyes and this madman bursts in.
Grabs me, throws me into the altar and...he set
the church on fire. Said he was gonna send us all
to Hell. Damned fool didn't count on him dying
first. The old timbers went up like matchsticks,
and the burning curtains fell on him.

ANTON
That seems just.

KURT
There was justice to be had that night, but that
wasn't it. So there I am, watching everything I'd
ever known burn around me...except it wasn't
just me. Five other priests, men who'd been my
friends all my life, and they were going to die
because of what I'd done.

ANTON
You did not set the fire.

KURT
Oh, I didn't strike the tinder, but I lit it all the
same. But I knew I had to get these men out. The
church was falling in on itself, and I just started
grabbing these men and dragging them out. The
last of them, my friend Gregor...I had him over
my shoulder and suddenly...

(KURT claps loudly)

KURT
A support beam comes crashing down. I managed
to toss him out the door, and then everything
went black. When I woke up, the church was gone

and my leg...crushed. Broken beyond repair. And that was justice, Anton.

KURT

ANTON

I do not understand.

KURT

God was punishing me for what I'd done. He could've killed me that night, but he's kinder than that, I suppose. Or crueler. Hard to tell sometimes. And so the church set me up here, tending to the dead. I've spent every day since that day cleaning the paths, reading the grave-stones and trying to drink away a life that I remember the way one remembers a story he was told long ago.

ANTON

Why did you tell me this?

(KURT is silent, thinking)

KURT

The day will come, Anton, where I will look God in the eye and have to answer for what I've done. I think it will be easier if I could...do something good again.

(ANTON rises)

KURT

You don't have to leave. I don't want you to.

ANTON

I'm not.

(ANTON begins to remove his bandages)

KURT

What are you doing?

ANTON
I said I would tell you about my face when you
told me about your leg.

KURT
You don't have to.

ANTON
Yes. I do.

*(He has unwrapped his face. It is a scarred & mangled
mess. KURT just stares at him)*

KURT
Oh my God.

ANTON
God had nothing to do with this.

*(KURT can only gape at ANTON. After a bit,
ANTON starts to leave)*

KURT
Don't go.

(ANTON stops, turns)

KURT
Whatever you've done...whatever's been done to
you...This is your home now, if you want it.

ANTON
I've never had a home.

KURT
"Never" is a lot like "always." It only exists until
it doesn't.

(Beat. ANTON shuts the door)

KURT
Good. I'm going to cook us up some supper. Sit

down already.

(ANTON sits. KURT begins to re-assemble his shack)

KURT
Where the hell did you throw my beans?

(ANTON begins to wrap his face again. KURT speaks without looking at him)

KURT
Put those down. You don't need them here.

(ANTON leaves his face unwrapped. Lights fade)

Scene Two

(The cemetery at night. KURT walks in holding a lantern. He makes sure no one is present, then motions ANTON to enter. ANTON, no longer bandaged, enters)

KURT
How does it feel?

ANTON
Strange.

KURT
To be out in the open, as you are?

ANTON
Yes. I feel...taller? I am unsure...

KURT
Christ, don't get any taller on me. I already need a damn ladder to look you in the eye.

ANTON
I am so used to hiding myself. When I went

unmasked before, the result was…violent.

KURT
You never need to worry about that here. Here, it's just me and buried bones.

ANTON
I like your company…and theirs…more than any other.

KURT
You can still do your work at night, but without them rags on your face. This is your graveyard now as much as it's mine.

ANTON
Perhaps more so. I do more work than you.

(KURT stares at him)

KURT
You just made a joke, didn't you?

ANTON
I did.

(KURT laughs, claps him on the back)

KURT
Ha! Not bad, lummox! Not bad.

ANTON
Thank you. Runt.

KURT
What?

ANTON
If you can call me "lummox," I can call you "runt."

KURT
I'm not a runt! You're just enormous! Everything
looks smaller to you.

(ANTON wanders around)

ANTON
It is so beautiful here.

KURT
You think so?

ANTON
I do. There is such order to these grave markers.
Like a garden of stone. And the trees that guard
over them. And the moonlight shining between
the branches, making paths of light in the mist.
It is so quiet...and so alive.

KURT
Not many'd say that about this place.

ANTON
They do not see it as I do. You cannot see the
dead here, just the growing, living things. The
trees, and the vines, and the birds that sing at
night. It is perfect.

KURT
I never saw it that way.

ANTON
Do you now?

(A breeze blows in, moving the mist. ANTON feels
it against his face. The emotion is almost too much)

KURT
Cold wind. Might be another storm coming.
Come on.

(He tries to move ANTON, who stands still, savoring the wind)

KURT
We should get inside.

ANTON
No.

KURT
You want to get thunderstruck? Tall as you are, you…

ANTON
I do not fear lightning or thunder. I…I can feel the wind on my face.

KURT
So can I, so let's just…

ANTON
Is this God?

(KURT stops, sees ANTON enjoying the moment, and closes his eyes, trying to do the same)

ANTON
What do you feel?

KURT
Nothing.

ANTON
Here. What do you feel here?

(ANTON taps KURT's chest)

KURT
I don't…

ANTON
The breath of God. Life. It is all around us.

KURT
How do you know?

ANTON
I just know.

(Beat. ANTON can tell something is upsetting KURT)

ANTON
Kurt? What is it?

KURT
Nothing. Let's go inside.

ANTON
I am your friend, yes?

KURT
Yes.

ANTON
If I have upset you...

KURT
You didn't upset me, I just...

(Beat)

KURT
When the wind blows, all I feel is the wind. But you stand here and talk of God and...you have no idea. Do you know what I would give to feel God's presence again?

ANTON
You were a priest.

KURT
And a poor one at that. Since the day God took my leg and my church...he wants nothing to do

with me. He turned his back, I turned mine, and that was that.

ANTON
A man burned your church. You tried to stop him.

KURT
And I'm sure the ashes thank me for my efforts.

(He pulls the old rosary out of his pocket)

KURT
You see this? This is all I have left of that place. Back then, when my thoughts turned dark, all I had to do was hold this, look at this...and it was as though God was taking my hand, consoling me. Now...now it's just cold, dead wood.

ANTON
Then why do you still have it?

(They are quiet for a moment)

KURT
Enough of this standing around. My leg's locking up.

(He turns to go)

ANTON
May I stay here, just a while longer?

KURT
We have no graves to dig tonight.

ANTON
I know. I just...I am happy here. I want to stay.

KURT
I said this was your home, didn't I? Don't have

to ask my permission. You want to stay, stay, you
lummox.

ANTON
Thank you. Runt.

(They smile at each other, and laugh a little.
KURT heads off. ANTON sits, listening to the
night birds sing. He whistles, trying to mimic their
calls. NADYA approaches from the darkness)

NADYA
Trying to speak to birds? I wonder what they
think you said.

(ANTON rises, stares at her)

ANTON
Nadya.

NADYA
Salutari, Anton.

ANTON
What are you doing here?

NADYA
I came to warn you.

(He stares at her, confused)

NADYA
There are worse things in this cemetery than you
and I this night.

(Lights fade)

Scene Three

(The shack. VICTOR stands warming his hands at the stove. His back is to the door. He wears a high-collared coat & a hat, so his face is obscured. KURT enters & sees him)

KURT
Hey! Hey! Who the hell are you?! Get out of my...

(VICTOR turns to him)

KURT
Wait...I know you, don't I?

VICTOR
We worked together, after a fashion, a year ago.

KURT
You...you're that doctor, yes?

KURT
Victor.

KURT
Christ, you're the one I dug up the corpses for.

VICTOR
Yes. That's why I'm here, in fact.

KURT
No. No no no. I told you then what I'm telling you now.

VICTOR
Listen to me.

KURT
I'm not pulling another pour soul out of the earth for you. Never again.

(VICTOR smiles)

VICTOR
That's just it, though. They don't have souls. That was the mistake I made. There's no equation for it, no chemical formula...that part of them is gone forever.

KURT
What are you talking about?

VICTOR
Our child has come home, Mr. Volker.

(KURT stares at him)

VICTOR
I made life, with your help.

KURT
Didn't your pa ever talk to you? I'm certain there has to be a lady involved somewhere.

VICTOR
What I did goes far beyond impregnating some girl. I made life...I...

(KURT grabs VICTOR's arm)

KURT
I don't know what you're talking about. I don't want to know. Just get out before I toss you out.

VICTOR
Why do you think I asked for parts instead of entire bodies? I wanted the strongest arms, the sharpest eyes, the fiercest heart...each individual piece had to be perfect. But their sum total was...abominable.

KURT
Get yourself to an inn and sleep it off.

VICTOR
And now that abomination is here.

(VICTOR pulls a gun from his belt, checking it. KURT freezes)

VICTOR
Calm yourself. I won't hurt you.

KURT
You've got a gun.

VICTOR
The bullet isn't for you. Sit.

(KURT sits)

VICTOR
You were a priest, yes? Or something of the sort. I think I remember you saying that once.

KURT
Yes.

VICTOR
Can you still absolve a man of his sins?

(Beat. KURT's demeanor softens)

KURT
No. That part of my life died a long time ago.

VICTOR
What if...could you try?

KURT
I'm sorry. That's not how it works.

(VICTOR sits, his emotions rising)

VICTOR
I never wanted to hurt anyone. You have to believe me.

KURT
All right.

VICTOR
The work I was doing...it was to preserve life. Perhaps indefinitely. And it...I don't know how it became what it became.

KURT
Doctor, I...

VICTOR
Victor. Please.

KURT
Victor. You're seeking absolution from a man... and not much of a man at that. My days in the confessional are long behind me.

VICTOR
Just hear me out. I beg of you.

(VICTOR collects himself)

VICTOR
Mr. Volker, when a child is born...naturally, as God intended, they have time to grow, to learn and adapt. I think...I think this is how a soul is formed. But my creature lacked all of that. It began its existence fully formed, in a body stronger than any ten men, but with an emotional capacity no greater than an infant's. Do you understand what I'm saying?

KURT
I'm sorry, I don't.

VICTOR
A baby is upset, it lashes out. But it is small, fragile...it can harm no one. Now, imagine that blind emotion, pure and unfettered by thought, but with the strength of a giant behind it.

(KURT begins to understand)

KURT
What?

VICTOR
I fled from it. I saw it rise up, saw its scarred and mangled face...its dead, soulless eyes...and I ran. I left it to the world in hopes that it would sputter out and die. But it didn't die. It endured, in a world that offered it nothing but hate. And so it became as monstrous within as it was without. It tracked me down and...

(Beat)

VICTOR
It killed my brother first. William. No more than 10 years old, and it snapped his neck, for no other reason beyond bringing me anguish. My servant Justine was next. Then ...my friend Henry, a man who'd never hurt any living being...dead. My servants, dead. My father and...and my wife...my beautiful Elizabeth...I saw him. Standing over her broken body, pointing at it as he glared at me. But he left me alive...always alive to suffer his wrath. I have hunted him these long months, and my hunt has led me here. I have come to warn you. The creature...

KURT
Anton.

VICTOR
What?

KURT
His name is Anton. And he is that man no longer.

VICTOR
You know him?

KURT
He is my friend.

(VICTOR grabs him, lifting him up)

VICTOR
What? What did you say?

KURT
Please...he's not the way he was. He's found peace here.

VICTOR
He has deceived you! He is as clever as he is
savage.

KURT
He came here to die! He wanted to die. That's
what he said. But...no, what he really wanted
was hope. Friendship.

(VICTOR releases him)

KURT
I'm sorry for what he's done to you. I am. No
man should ever suffer like that. But I'm telling you, if you leave...if you let him go...he'll
never hurt another soul again.

*(Beat. VICTOR considers this, then points his gun
at KURT)*

VICTOR
I'm afraid I can't take that chance.

(Lights fade)

SCENE FOUR

(The cemetery, with ANTON & NADYA, shortly after we saw them last)

NADYA
So this is your face.

ANTON
Yes.

NADYA
Would you...can I touch it?

ANTON
Why would you do that?

NADYA
I am curious.

ANTON
The last time you laid your hands on me, you ran in fear.

NADYA
I know.

ANTON
I am not inclined to trust you now.

NADYA
How could I hurt you?

ANTON
You have already hurt me. Deeply. I have no
desire to experience it again.

(She lowers her head, ashamed)

ANTON
You came to warn me? Then do so and be gone.

NADYA
There is a man in Ingolstadt. He is hunting you.

ANTON
I am no stranger to that.

NADYA
He's your father.

(Beat)

ANTON
What did you say?

NADYA
About this tall. Dark hair, wild eyes. He came to
me last night, paid me to read his future. To help
him find you.

ANTON
And you did this?

(She says nothing. He grabs her arm)

ANTON
Did you tell my father I was here!?

(She pushes him away)

NADYA
I live in filth! I have no family anymore, no friends! Only men who would see their future or see up my skirts! And this man...he offered me more gold than I could earn in a year!

ANTON
You have betrayed me.

NADYA
Yes, dammit. And I am trying to make it right.

ANTON
Why?! What do you care if he finds me, if he ends my life? I am only a monster to you!

NADYA
Stop attacking me! I...

(ANTON closes on her quickly. She falls backward, terrified)

ANTON
I have not attacked you yet, little gypsy. You should know this because you are still breathing.

NADYA
I'm sorry for what I said to you...what I did to you. I am!

ANTON
Your word means less than nothing.

NADYA
He told me what you did. The people you killed. His brother. His wife.

(ANTON backs off)

NADYA
You may look down your crooked nose at me, but you are no innocent. You've bloodied your hands more in a year than I could in a lifetime.

ANTON
I am trying to be something better than I was! I have left behind man's world and entombed myself here!

NADYA
I have travelled further than you can imagine, and this much I know; unless you flee to the frozen North itself, you will never be free of men.

(Beat)

NADYA
The doctor said he had business to attend to, someone he had to warn about you. Do you know what that means?

ANTON
No.

NADYA
It means you can leave here, tonight, and be gone before he finds you. That is what I came here to say.

ANTON
First you sell me to my enemy, now you would aid in my escape?

NADYA
Do not presume to know my mind.

ANTON
This is my home.

NADYA
Then it is good there are many graves here, for the doctor will likely put you in one. *(She crosses away)* I have done what I came to do. Flee or die; the choice is yours.

ANTON
I should break your neck. I have done worse for less.

(She pulls her knife)

NADYA
Try it and I'll cut your throat.

ANTON
You can try.

NADYA
Stay back.

(She starts to flee, but ANTON grabs her. She tries to stab him, but he catches the knife and lifts her high. She cries out in pain)

ANTON
You were the only woman who ever looked at me with kindness. I should have known better than to trust you.

NADYA
Let me go!

ANTON
Why? So you can cut my throat?

NADYA
I won't hurt you! Please!

ANTON
We are far past begging, Nadya.

(He squeezes her wrist until she drops the knife. She cries out again)

ANTON
A part of me loved you the minute I saw you. You are very beautiful, and I wanted to be close to that beauty.

NADYA
You still can be.

ANTON
You say that only to save your life. I can hear the lie in your voice.

NADYA
I'm not lying.

(He grabs her hair, pulling her face to his)

ANTON
Look at me! Would you have these dead lips kiss you? These patchwork hands caress you? Or does your bile rise to be this close to my face?

(She leans forward and kisses him. He releases her, and backs away, confused & perhaps afraid)

NADYA
I could run from you now, but I am still here. There is no gain in this for me.

ANTON
Why...?

NADYA
Because I have hurt you. Because I will not do it again.

(She walks to him. He backs away)

NADYA
Stop.

ANTON
What do you...?

NADYA
Anton. Stop.

(He does. She reaches up slowly and puts her hands on his face)

NADYA
This face is not so bad a face.

(He takes her hands and begins to weep. She squeezes his hands)

ANTON
I was going to kill you.

NADYA
No.

ANTON
I had my hands around your throat.

NADYA
You lashed against one who had hurt you. But no, you would not have killed me. You are that man no longer.

ANTON
How do you know?

NADYA
That man hid his face from the world. You have nothing to hide now.

(He looks around)

ANTON
I will be sad to leave this place.

NADYA
I am sorry that you must. But you found a piece of your soul here. Perhaps other pieces are out there, waiting.

(He rises)

ANTON
You kissed me.

NADYA
Yes. I...I think it was goodbye.

(He lowers his head)

ANTON
As do I.

(Lights fade)

Scene Five

(KURT's shack. It is dark. ANTON enters)

ANTON
Kurt?

(No answer)

ANTON
If you are asleep, I am sorry to wake you but...

(A match is struck, and a candle lit. VICTOR is illuminated by its light. ANTON stands very still. VICTOR points the pistol at him)

ANTON
Father.

VICTOR
Do not move. Do not think of moving. Am I understood?

ANTON
I do not fear you.

VICTOR
I don't need your fear. I need your acquiescence.

ANTON
Where is Kurt?

VICTOR
He is safe. If you wish him to remain thus, you will do as I say. Sit.

ANTON
If you have harmed him...

VICTOR
I said sit.

(ANTON just glares at him, then sits)

VICTOR
Can you sense it, in the dark? The hatred between us clings to the air like a cold mist.

ANTON
What do you want, father?

VICTOR
Don't call me that! I am not your father!

ANTON
If not you, then who?

VICTOR
You are the Devil's orphan, if you are anything at all.

ANTON
God and the Devil...I thought you put no stake in such things.

VICTOR
My perspective has grown since you destroyed

my life.

(He pushes a glass towards ANTON)

ANTON
What is this?

VICTOR
If you wish to see the gravedigger again, you will drink.

(ANTON suddenly rises, grabbing VICTOR by the throat)

VICTOR
Kill me and you'll never know where I hid Mr. Volker. He'll die of his wounds unless I tend to them.

(ANTON lets him go)

VICTOR
I have every advantage now. Even if you kill me, you're only bringing me peace. But for your friend's sake, quench your thirst.

(ANTON takes the cup)

ANTON
You mean to poison me.

VICTOR
I mean to drug you, actually. Poison would end this too quickly.

(ANTON stares at the cup)

VICTOR
I had to guess at the dosage, considering your distinct metabolism. But I am confident that the contents of that cup will weaken your body

without dulling your mind too much. I want you
awake for what comes next.

ANTON
What does come next?

VICTOR
Put cup to lip and find out.

(ANTON stares at the cup for a bit, then drinks)

VICTOR
You willingly cripple yourself, for the sake of a
drunken wretch you barely know?

ANTON
He is my friend.

VICTOR
You are a collection of corpses, somewhere
between a charnel pit and a butcher's floor. You
have no friends.

(ANTON staggers a bit)

VICTOR
And so the chemicals do their work. Don't bother
fighting them.

ANTON
I have..fought...all my life.

VICTOR
No one knows that better than I.

(VICTOR checks the gun)

VICTOR
I thought I wouldn't be able to control myself
when I saw you again. I have a great desire to
revenge myself upon you but...you have no idea.

No idea of the time, the resources, my very lifeblood....all these things I poured into your creation. You were meant to be the greatest scientific achievement mankind ever witnessed. I want very much to know what went wrong.

ANTON
You will never know.

VICTOR
Don't be petulant, beast. Let your death mean something.

ANTON
I have...no answers...for you.

VICTOR
You are in many ways a perfect being. Stronger than any man before you; Senses sharper than any animal's. And your mind...I put within your misshapen skull the mind of a genius. And yet here you are, a rag-covered madman. What a waste.

(He grabs ANTON's face roughly)

VICTOR
Why did you become this demon?! What turned you into this?

ANTON
You.

(VICTOR backs away)

ANTON
For most of my short life...I wanted only one thing. Your love. Even...when you abandoned me...I wanted to know you. A father's love...all any child wants.

VICTOR
Quiet.

ANTON
You gave me...only hate. I took that hate, and
put it in the place...where my soul should have
been.

(VICTOR sets the gun down)

VICTOR
I am sorry. Sorry that I ever made you. Sorry
that you lived long enough to become this...
thing. Sorry that yours has been a life of unend-
ing horror. But I have paid for my mistakes.
You have to pay for yours. Do you understand
that?

ANTON
I do not know. After all...I have done...it seems
that you should kill me. But for the first time...I
do not wish to die.

(Beat)

VICTOR
The answers I seek...I'll never find them, will
I?

ANTON
I do not know.

VICTOR
I just...if I could make some sense of this,
everything that has happened, perhaps then I
would...I suppose it doesn't matter, in the end.

ANTON
Is this the end?

VICTOR
Yes. I believe it is.

(VICTOR rises, crosses to ANTON & puts the gun to his head)

ANTON
Wait.

VICTOR
No.

ANTON
My friend...please let me see my friend.

VICTOR
I owe you nothing.

ANTON
You owe me everything! I exist only because of you!

VICTOR
You won't trick me again.

ANTON
Please! I beg of you! Just let me tell him goodbye!

(Beat. VICTOR lowers the gun)

VICTOR
It seems there's still something human left inside me.

(VICTOR leaves. ANTON tries to stand, succeeds in doing so, but is still very weak. He flops back into the chair. VICTOR soon returns with KURT, bound and gagged and injured)

ANTON
Kurt...

VICTOR
Here. Say your goodbyes.

(He throws KURT into the chair)

ANTON
I thought...you left him near death.

VICTOR
A small lie will be the least of my sins.

(VICTOR ungags KURT)

KURT
Untie me, you whore-son!

ANTON
Kurt...

KURT
I'll rip your throat out with my teeth!

ANTON
Kurt, listen to me.

KURT
Has that bastard hurt you?

ANTON
A sedative only.

KURT
Christ, I'm glad to hear that.

ANTON
You have to listen...

KURT
I'll get us out of this, boy. Trust me. I...

ANTON
Thank you, Kurt.

KURT
Don't thank me yet.

ANTON
Thank you...for teaching me...everything that
was worth knowing.

KURT
What?

ANTON
These past weeks...I have become something...
better than I was. Because of you.

KURT
What are you saying?

(ANTON smiles)

ANTON
Goodbye.

(VICTOR closes on him, gun to his head)

KURT
No!

VICTOR
Close your eyes, Mr. Volker.

ANTON
Kurt, it's all right.

KURT
I'll give you anything!

(VICTOR just stares at him)

KURT
What do you want?! If I don't have it, I'll get it!
Just don't hurt him!

VICTOR
It's true then. You care for each other.

KURT
I don't want to see him die and I don't want to
see you damned.

VICTOR
My damnation is foregone at this point. But...

(VICTOR circles behind ANTON)

VICTOR
I have an idea, beast. You were right about me,
partially at any rate. I never taught you anything.
Every lesson you learned, you learned at the
boot heel of the world. But now I can show you
something important, before you cease to be.

(VICTOR pulls a long knife from his belt)

ANTON
What...?

VICTOR
This? This is to slit your throat in a moment.

ANTON
But...the pistol...

VICTOR
The pistol isn't for you anymore.

(He points it at KURT)

KURT
Christ!

ANTON
NO!

VICTOR
You have murdered every single person I ever cared about. I will show you what that feels like.

(ANTON lurches up but stumbles. VICTOR kicks him hard)

VICTOR
The pain you've lived with all your life? It is nothing compared to this lesson I give to you.

(He fires. ANTON lurches up, clenching his fist in front of KURT. VICTOR just stares, shocked. When ANTON opens his fist, a metal ball drops from his hand)

ANTON
The dosage was not correct, father.

(VICTOR lunges at ANTON with the knife. ANTON grabs him, slamming him into the wall. He cries out)

KURT
Anton! Don't!

ANTON
You would have killed the only person who ever showed me kindness, and called it justice?

VICTOR
...burn in hell...

(ANTON slams him again)

ANTON
You said if I killed you, you would be at peace? Let us see.

(ANTON puts a hand on VICTOR's head begins to squeeze)

KURT
Stop it!

ANTON
Soon your fragile skull will break, father, and I will be free of you at last.

KURT
Stop!

ANTON
You should not have hurt my friend.

KURT
STOP!

(ANTON turns, stares at KURT)

KURT
God almighty...you say you regret the things you've done? Then please...please, don't do them again.

ANTON
He has to die!

(ANTON turns back to VICTOR, begins to squeeze again. VICTOR cries out)

KURT
You're a better man than this, Anton.

ANTON
I am not a man!

KURT
You are. You are a man, a good man...and my friend.

(ANTON is about to kill VICTOR, but stops. He drops him. They are all still in tense exhaustion, then VICTOR raises his knife. ANTON hits him and he flies into the wall, then lies unconscious. ANTON takes his knife and cuts KURT's bonds)

KURT
Anton, you didn't...?

ANTON
He still lives.

(KURT checks on VICTOR)

ANTON
You did not believe me?

KURT
Had to be sure. Give me the rope.

(ANTON tosses it to him, and KURT begins to tie up VICTOR. ANTON collapses into a chair)

KURT
You all right?

ANTON
No. But I will live.

(KURT goes to him)

KURT
What do we do now?

(ANTON looks up at him. Lights fade)

Scene Six

(The graveyard. No one is there. KURT walks in, making sure the place is empty. Once he's satisfied it is, he heads over to the grave ANTON emerged from in Act I. He hollers loudly at the dirt)

KURT
All's clear!

(The earth shifts, and ANTON rises from the ground. He shakes off the dirt)

KURT
You're quite a sight.

ANTON
So I've been told. The policemen?

KURT
Gone. Took the doctor with them.

ANTON
What did you tell them?

KURT
The truth, more or less. The doctor came in,
raving. Attacked me. I managed to fight him off.

ANTON
That's not the truth. I am the one who fought
him.

KURT
I could've taken him out if you hadn't gotten
there first.

ANTON
I think you are wrong.

KURT
Pfft. What do you know?

ANTON
I know what "embellishment" means.

(KURT chuckles)

KURT
You're getting a feeling for jokes.

ANTON
I am learning.

KURT
That was a fancy trick, by the way. Catching that
bullet.

ANTON
I am faster than most.

KURT
Thank you.

ANTON
For being fast?

KURT
For saving my life, you lummox.

ANTON
Had I not come here, your life would never have
been in danger.

KURT
I don't care about the whys and wherefores. I'm
just...thank you.

ANTON
You are welcome.

(Beat)

KURT
The doctor kept mum about you.

ANTON
I thought as much. He wants to kill me himself.

KURT
Maybe he'll stop now.

ANTON
No. He will never stop. All I have done is gained
a little time.

KURT
All right then. What will you do with that time?

(Beat)

ANTON
I have to leave, Kurt.

KURT
No you don't.

ANTON
I do. You know I do.

KURT
Because of that doctor? Who knows how long they'll put him behind bars? He attacked a priest!

ANTON
A former priest.

KURT
Still pretty bad.

ANTON
He will escape. He will hunt me until he is dead. And...I no longer have it in me to kill him.

KURT
I think maybe you never did.

ANTON
I did. Before I came here, before I met you... murder came as easily to me as breathing.

KURT
I want you to stay.

ANTON
As do I. But where I am, no one is safe. Tonight taught me that.

KURT
Where would you go then? There are people... well, everywhere.

ANTON
North.

KURT
There are people North.

ANTON
Not to the farthest North.

(KURT just stares at him)

ANTON
I have a friend...a gypsy. She told me that it would be the only place free of mankind. I will go there.

KURT
What if the doctor follows?

ANTON
He will. But this time, there will be no one he can use against me.

KURT
This is your home.

ANTON
And no matter how far I go, I will always think of it that way.

(Beat)

KURT
The doctor told me something. I think you need to know.

ANTON
What?

KURT
Do you know why you came here?

ANTON
To this graveyard?

KURT
Yes.

ANTON
I was lost, wandering. I found myself here.

KURT
I think it's more than that.

(Beat)

KURT
I know what you are. A man made from the parts
of others.

ANTON
Yes.

KURT
This is where those parts came from.

(ANTON stares at him)

KURT
A year ago, this young doctor came to me, offered
me a bag of gold for dead bodies. Or parts of 'em,
anyways.

ANTON
You are the one who found me?

KURT
Yes. I didn't know what the doctor was doing. It's
not so strange a thing, medical students paying for
fresh corpses. Had I known...

ANTON
I am alive because of you.

KURT
I suppose so.

ANTON
I have always thought of the doctor as my father.

KURT
All right.

ANTON
Does this make you my mother?

(Beat. KURT glares at ANTON, who starts to laugh. KURT does as well)

KURT
Christ, I'm glad I didn't have to nurse you!

(They both laugh more, letting it die out naturally. They enjoy the quiet night)

ANTON
I will miss you, gravedigger.

KURT
Wouldn't have to miss me if you just stayed, dammit.

ANTON
You understand that...

KURT
Yes, yes. I understand. I hate it, but I understand. Just doesn't seem fair.

ANTON
I know.

KURT
You've done bad things, but you were just a child then.

ANTON
It was not even a year ago.

KURT
You know what I mean.

ANTON
I know that...Kurt, I have a soul now. I did not

then, but I do now. Because of you.

KURT
I don't give souls, Anton. I just...helped you recognize it for what it was.

ANTON
No one has ever given me so much.

(He offers KURT his hand)

ANTON
Thank you.

(KURT takes it, then pulls him into a hug. After a bit, they let go)

KURT
Goodbye, lummox.

ANTON
Goodbye, my friend.

(ANTON exits. KURT watches him go, then takes his rosary out of his pocket. He looks at it, speaks to it)

KURT
Just...watch over him, all right?

(Nothing happens. He shakes his head, laughs at his foolishness. Then wind blows through the graveyard)

END OF PLAY

ABOUT THE PLAYWRIGHT

Joseph Zettelmaier is a Michigan-based playwright and four-time nominee for the Steinberg/ American Theatre Critics Association Award for best new play, first in 2006 for ALL CHILDISH THINGS, then in 2007 for LANGUAGE LESSONS, in 2010 for IT CAME FROM MARS and in 2012 for DEAD MAN'S SHOES. Other plays include SALVAGE, NORTHERN AGGRESSION, DR. SEWARD'S DRACULA, ALL CHILDISH THINGS, INVASIVE SPECIES, DEAD MAN'S SHOES, THE SCULLERY MAID, NIGHT BLOOMING and EBENEZER.

POINT OF ORIGIN won Best Locally Created Script 2002 from the Ann Arbor News, and THE STILLNESS BETWEEN BREATHS also won Best New Play 2005 from the Oakland Press. THE STILLNESS BETWEEN BREATHS and IT CAME FROM MARS were selected to appear in the National New Play Network's Festival of New Plays. He also co-authored Flyover, USA:Voices From Men of the Midwest at the Williamston Theatre (Winner of the 2009 Thespie Award for Best New Script). He adapted CHRISTMAS CAROL'D for the Performance Network.

IT CAME FROM MARS was a recipient of 2009's Edgerton Foundation New American Play Award, and won Best New Script 2010 from the Lansing State Journal. His play DEAD MAN'S SHOES won the Edgerton Foundation New American Play Award in 2011. He is an Associate Artist at First Folio Shakespeare, an Artistic Ambassador to the National New Play Network, and an adjunct lecturer at Eastern Michigan University, where he teaches Dramatic Composition.

MORE PLAYS FROM SORDELET INK

A TALE OF TWO CITIES
by Christoper M Walsh
adapted from the novel by Charles Dickens

THE COUNT OF MONTE CRISTO
by Christoper M Walsh
adapted from the novel by Alexandre Dumas

THE MOONSTONE
by Robert Kauzlaric
adapted from the novel by Wilkie Collins

HER MAJESTY'S WILL
by Robert Kauzlaric
adapted from the novel by David Blixt

SEASON ON THE LINE
by Shawn Pfautsch
adapted from Herman Melville's MOBY-DICK

HATFIELD & McCOY
by Shawn Pfautsch

ONCE A PONZI TIME
by Joe Foust

EVE OF IDES
by David Blixt

VISIT WWW.SORDELETINK.COM FOR MORE!